LIKE THE WOMAN
AT THE WELL
HE WAITED ON ME

TRUE STORY OF A SINNER TURNED SAINT

I0086171

TOCCARRA JAMES

ISBN-13:
978-0692564097
(Empowered Me Publishing)

ISBN-10:
0692564098

Acknowledgements

This book is dedicated to my 2 children, King Redd III and JaCee Moore. To my nieces and nephews; Kadijah James, Kashontae James, Alvont Graham, Tymel James and the late Coreyon "JC" Graham. No matter how rough life appears to be; always pay your tithe, no matter what. Put God first even when it seems He is nowhere to be found as He will never leave you. Call on Him in trouble and "trust Him in Spirit and in Truth". Also, don't ever allow anyone to tell you what you can't do, push yourself to the limit. God has great things in store for you if you will allow him to use you. I pray daily that you guys stick together, no matter what. To Coreyon "JC" Graham (*June 12, 2000 – February 16, 2006*), I love you and miss you every day of my life. You would be so proud of your brother and cousins right now; they are really standing in the paint and thank you for teaching King to play football that day. That's all he wants to do now. We love you and miss you dearly.

Chapter 1
New Kid On The Block

From early on in life, I could tell that I was "different" than the other kids.   Too afraid to tell anyone in fear of them thinking I was crazy; I've always felt there was something in me that I could feel pulling on me and I could see things before they actually happened. I was and still is darker skinned then a lot of my peers and it was just a little harder for me to make friends. I've always felt singled out. I grew up in my grandma's home up until I was maybe ten or eleven because from what I understood, my mom was in school and working a lot. We didn't have a lot of nice toys and video games as my grandma did the best she could to raise us. I remember one time I fell asleep on the school bus, but because Wildwood is so small, everyone knows everyone. The school bus driver and my grandma were friends and she knew where I lived. She called my grandma and said "Carra fell asleep on the bus, do you need me to bring her home or can you stop by and get her?"   My grandma told her to drop me off on her way home. I was so scared I was going to get in trouble because my grandma was very stern but instead she just laughed. When my mom finished school years later, she came to get us and we moved to Belleview, Florida. We lived in a single wide trailer. It was my two sisters, my mom and I. I remember I use to roll up newspaper or brown paper bags from the grocery store, put tape on it and tried to smoke it. I was only doing it because I saw the actors smoking on TV. I almost died when I inhaled that mess. We later moved to Lowell, FL to be closer to my mom's job. We actually lived in a sub division of houses on the actual prison ground. My cousin whom we didn't get to play with much in my younger years lived next to us so that was the highlight of my life. On top of all that, I was starting middle school!

Middle School was all I heard about from my older sister. I wasn't her nor did I have her outgoing personality so I wondered how this was going to work out for me. She was really cool, fare skinned, nicely shaped, and knew how to do her hair. I was dark skinned, couldn't dress, wore my hair the same way every day, and was scared to speak to people. Although I had my cousin with me, I was still intimidated. My cousin knew everyone because her and my Aunt lived on the prison grounds longer than we had so she was comfortable at school and I was the new kid on the block. I was a prime target and easily picked on and made fun of. Because I had never been exposed to anything like this, I was a wreck and hated going to this middle school I had heard so much about. The thing that drove girls crazy was their new boyfriends; however, I couldn't pay a boy to look at me let alone like me as a girlfriend. When we finally moved; we took up residence in a couple others places before finally ending up in Silver Spring Shores, FL which is still in Marion County. I was little older I think maybe thirteen or fourteen and was getting a little better at meeting people. I had my first boyfriend who turned out not to be all I heard about. He eventually threw me under the bus by telling me his ex-girlfriend "Samantha" wanted to fight me. *Why does fighting have to play a role in every situation* I thought to myself. However, I knew I was not trying to be picked on in my new surroundings so I asked him to tell me more about her and he offered to take me to her house. I hopped on the handle bars of his bike and took the twenty minute ride to her house. Looking through the path as we approached her house; I could see a lot of people in her yard and I could see cars and hear laughter and then we stopped. He said "there she is right there" and pointed her out. I then hopped off the bike and begin to walk up to her house. My boyfriend stayed in the path on the bike that we rode through to get there. As I walked up to her, she was surrounded by her boyfriend, some other guys, and a couple females smoking weed and Newport Cigarettes. I said "hey, which one of yall is Samantha?" She said "that's me." I said "my name is Carra and Mike told me you wanted to fight me." She said "he told me you wanted to fight me, I don't even know you!" I then turned to the bushes where he was still sitting on the bike and called for him to come to me. He slowly exited the bushes and when he got close enough to hear what I was going to say to him I said "why you lied and said this girl wanted to fight me?" He chuckled and said "I didn't know you was gone want me to bring you to her house!" We both cursed him out and nearly fought him. He then turned and rode off on the bike leaving me to her house and just like that, Samantha and I were friends. She even offered me to smoke some weed and a Newport cigarette with her. This was my first time smoking weed or a real cigarette (remember the brown paper bag experience) Again, I didn't want to seem like a lame so there I was smoking for the first time. In hindsight, God was showing grace even then because He knew I surely wasn't prepared to fight this girl. He also knew that it was not a wise decision to go to someone's house to fight them and had the police been called, I was going to jail. I was in the wrong place at the wrong time. When God places us in certain situations, very often they are never meant to harm us, they are only meant to show us His Glory which is "made perfect in weakness" His grace is surely sufficient (2nd Corinthians 12:9 NLT).

Chapter 2
Then Comes Love

We had begun to settle into "The Shores" and get acclimated and comfortable and I was beginning to unravel and come out of my cocoon. I had made more friends and the count of them was more than enemies which was never the case in the old neighborhoods and schools. I then met a girl name "Moesha" who was very popular in general but even more popular with the guys. I didn't know at the time what it meant to be so popular with the guys so I was interested. Her and Samantha knew each other but did not hang in the same circle of friends. Samantha and I had become so close we were now best friends. Everywhere you saw her, you saw me. I also wanted to know more about Moesha's life style, it again just seemed interesting. On top of all that; she also smoked weed and could get it real easy. One day Moesha and I were chilling and she asked me if I wanted to go to Wild Waters which was a water theme park. Everybody was going. It was the summer and the park ran specials during the summer. It sounded like fun and so we went. We got to the park and just like she said before we got there, it was jammed packed! I had never been there and it was so much to see. All the girls had on these two- piece bikinis and there were so many dudes, I had never in my life seen anything like it! We walked around surveying the area to see if we could find any of our friends from school. It was great! It was a rush! We finally bumped into a friend who had some weed so we found a corner and smoked out. This friend was also with one of Moesha's guy friends and as they begin to chop it up, she introduced me. She said "this is my friend from school, Toccarra" and he said "my name Cory". I said "hey" in a calm way but inside I was giggling to myself and thinking this dude is real nice. We sat there for another twenty minutes or so and then we walked off to go and enjoy the park. We rode rides, flirted, ate, sat, and rode rides until we had enough. When we got back to her house, she asked me to stay the night and I agreed to stay. I was so tired and still amazed at how many people was at the park. I had never seen anything like it. I was finally getting out with friends and doing fun stuff. I wasn't quite comfortable yet; however it was fun and my adrenaline was rushing. Once we showered, ate and started to lounge, I noticed her walls in her room were filled with posters of rappers and hand writing of things she liked. My room at my house was so bare and bland. Compared to hers, it looked like a room no one slept in. As I continued to glance at her wall, I noticed a few hand written lists with names and numbers on them. I look down the list and whose name and number do I see? Yep, Cory from the theme park. I asked about him and she said he was friends with her uncle. She asked, "Why, do you like him?" I replied, "He cute." "Write his number down then and call him." She replied back. I really didn't want to seem too eager. "Umm ok, I will before I leave tomorrow." As soon as she left the room I wrote his number down! A couple days after that, without even thinking about what I was getting ready to do, I called him. He answered the phone and said "Hello" and I said "Hello, can I speak to Cory?" "This me, who is this?" He replied. "This is Toccarra, I met you at Wild Waters with Moesha." "Oh okay, how you got my number?" He asked. I just laughed. We spoke for a while and while talking, I got up the nerve to ask if I could come to his house. He replied,

"You don't know where I live." I hung the phone up and was at his front door in less than twenty minutes WALKING! I was all giggly on the inside. He was blown away needless to say. He invited me in and we smoke some weed in his garage and talked until the sun came up. Over the next few months, we begin to get thick and started to build a relationship to the point where we became inseparable. I didn't want to be away from him and he didn't want to be away from me. I then began to sneak out of the window to see him. This was an easy task because my mom worked the graveyard shift. When she left at 11:30 pm, I would wait a while to be sure she was gone and then out the window I would go. I would always leave it cracked just enough to get back in. For about four or five months that worked until one night the window was completely closed when I tried to get back in. Because I shared a room with my baby sister, I pecked on it a couple times and nothing. I did it again and nothing and again and nothing. I went around the house to the side door to enter the living room and my mom's car was sitting in the carport. I knew this was not going to turn out good. To make matters worse, the door was cracked open and the TV was on. It was about 5 am and I been gone since about midnight. I pushed the door open and she turned with a wet face, a Virginia Slim cigarette in her mouth, and told me to get out! She came toward me, gave me a $5.00 bill, handed me a bag of clothes that was sitting by the front door and showed me the door! I took the clothes and turned to the door sobbing and walked out. What the heck was I going to do now? She closed the door behind me. I stood there crying for a while but the door never opened. I started walking and headed to the corner store by Cory's house and called his cell. By this time he was at work and he answered "What's up?" "My mama was home and she just put me out." I was crying uncontrollably. "I'm on my way." He replied. He came and picked me up and we went down the road to this lake near his house to wrap our heads around what was going on and what the heck we were going to do. We were hesitant to go to his house because his parents who were elderly in age lived there. Being that I was only sixteen and Cory was twenty three; we knew they were going to think something wasn't quite right. Cory finally got up the courage to walk in his house and ask his mom if I could stay for a couple days. When I walked in they immediately knew I was young but didn't know how young. We lied and told them I was eighteen. They agreed but made it clear that it was only temporary. A month or so later I still hadn't gone home and I was getting comfortable being out on my own. I was even beginning to think about going to an alternative school because high school, which I would skip on regular, was just not for me; it interfered with me getting high. What an idiot huh? Cory would take me to my sister's house for school and I started to skip school AGAIN. I remember one particular day a friend and I skipped school to get high. She was driving and we were on the back streets of Ocala with the music blasting and singing along. The next thing I knew, a F250 dooly truck t-boned the car on my side. I remember being unconscious. When I woke up, I was in the hospital but was soon released to my mom with a concussion. God's intention was never to kill me. As I often have said and will say; "His grace is sufficient". I am convinced He did want to scare some sense back into me. He saw the road that I was traveling on. I just didn't see it. After that, I went back to Cory's house to get my head right. One day as I was going to get my nails done, as soon as I sat in the nail techs chair; in walks my mom whom I hadn't seen since she put me out; except when the doctors released me to her after the truck hit us She quickly snatched me up and out of the nail shop and we headed back to her house. We sat and talked about where I had been all this time and she explained why she did what she did. I told her I had been staying at Cory's house and we begin to talk about him. I lied and told her he was eighteen because eighteen sounded much better dating a sixteen year old then twenty three years old. A month later she took me to the doctor to put me on birth control. It was at this time that I found out that I was six weeks pregnant. From the clinic we went straight to an abortion clinic in Gainesville, Fl. I wasn't even asked if this is what I wanted to do. While on the way there, she began to talk to me and tell me that she didn't want me ruining my life and that I would thank her later. After all, my sister had a daughter at an early age. When the procedure was over and I had awakened; she told me that I cried the whole time I was under anesthesia. She also told me that it was a girl. My daughter would have been nineteen years old had she been born. I was going to name her after Cory's grandma. I think about her all the time. I was crushed whole heartedly. I cried every day for about two months. The first time I saw Cory after the abortion occurred; I broke down again and couldn't control myself. I've never felt that kind of pain before. It wasn't a physical pain, it was an emotional pain that caused bitterness and resentment against my mom for the longest time. After the abortion, it really did something to me. The relationship between Cory and I ultimately ended eight years later but not before I conceived and delivered another child; a healthy baby boy named after him. There will be times in life when you are pushed out of relationships by God and you are not sure why. This was one I wanted to work but I just wasn't ready because I must admit; I was very immature. By the time I was mature and ready, the relationship itself wasn't ready as he had moved on. It just was not meant to be. God will place you in places for a season (Ecclesiastes 3:1-8 KJV). When He wants you out, He will close the door and no man, woman or child will open a door that God has closed. I don't care how many times you cry, jump on one foot and spin in a circle calling Jesus, Jesus, Jesus! How many things you break, how many times you both try and try to make it work, it will not work. It will be like a ram running its horns into a wall that was not ever meant to fall down. It's something that will have you scratching your head trying to make sense of but "*trust in the Lord with all your heart: do not depend on your own understanding*" (Proverbs 3:5 NLT).

Chapter 3
In The Meantime

The relationship was gone and I had been exposed to the "street life" and fooled around and got caught up. I started seeing the nice cars and clothes and saw my sister hanging out in a night club called "The Brown Derby" which was a scene I knew nothing about. She would wait until my mom was asleep at night, get me to help her push mom's car out of the drive way up the road, put it in neutral until it was down the hill, crank it up and off to the club she went. She would never let me go and would always tell me I was too young. Needless to say; by her telling me no, that just sparked my curiosity all the more. One night Samantha asked if I wanted to go to the "Café" which was also a club. I was so excited and we went. A lot of the people wore dresses that could've doubled as a shirt and dramatic make up which I knew nothing about. There was weed smoke everywhere in the air and people were just standing around in the parking lot listening to music. I thought to myself *is this what all the hype is about.* We hung out laughing, playing and smoking weed just like everyone else. With Samantha, I could be myself and just chill. It was always fun to be around her. Her family immediately accepted me just like I was a part of their family and still do to date. They always stood up for me no matter what! Right or wrong! Once the relationship with Cory was completely over, I left The Shores and moved in with my sister where I was attempting to go to school earlier. She lived in "Busbee Quarters" which was in the heart of Ocala. "Busbee Quarters" was a housing project for section 8 recipients. It was a party out there every day and that's where everybody that was somebody hung out. One night my sister was getting dressed to go to the club and I asked to go, she was like *"okay, put this on"* and threw me a dress. It was really tight. We then styled my hair to make me look a lot older. (It was a club for 21 and over). The club was called "Starlight Night Club" in Gainesville, FL. Once on the inside, I thought *this is nothing like The Café*. There were lights, loud music, girls grinding, flashes from a camera, and I was so nervous. We danced all night and I thought *I can get use to this.* For the next couple years that became my routine. Party from sun up till sun down and club like it was going out of style. The only time I didn't party was when I was pregnant. I remember when I was three months pregnant driving my mom's car and I passed out with my then four year old niece in the back seat. I was high on weed, it was the middle of summer, and I was headed back to my mom's house. I began sweating, feeling faint and passed out. I knew something was wrong. I was in the fast lane on SR40 trying to pull off on the left median. When I woke up I was in the parking lot of a business and my clothes were soaked with sweat. I wasn't able to put the car in park before I passed out, so I veered back into the left lane, then into the right lane, jumped the curb of the business, and ran head on into a concreate post that was also the street light. I awakened to paramedics on the scene and my mom who also had been notified. She came to the window and asked me if I was okay. I told her yes. I heard a cry from the floor board of the front passenger seat where my niece ended up. She was in the backseat before the accident. God had mercy on my life, the life of my unborn child, and my niece. A saying comes to my mind when I look back and think of what happened. Rev. Dr. Patricia Hauser says *"A lot of times when our lives are spared, it is not spared for us, it is spared for someone else.*" We all walked away from that accident without a scratch. Had God chosen to take my life that day; my child could have possibly died and I wouldn't have my now seven year old son. Glory be to God!!!

Chapter 4
After The Pain

After I delivered my oldest son, I was back to what I learned how to do best; partying and making money. There was really nothing wrong with it in my eyes because I was good at it. It just made sense then. I also started to hang with a guy my sister was dating name "Jason". Jason and I had one thing in common; we both knew how to make money. He was cool and always had some of the best weed. One day he had to go and take my sister to work but there was a little problem. He had two rental cars that needed to be back on the lot or else he would be charged late fees. Because my sister would normally be the one to drive one of the rentals, he was in a dilemma because he was taking her to work. I volunteered to ride with my sister to her job and he would follow and then once she got to work we would drop her off and I would drive the rental car back. Well, the car was a F150 truck and that was my first time driving a truck! Super nervous but excited! She pulled up in front of the store where she worked and got out and I hopped in the driver seat, put the truck in drive and pulled off. To exit the parking lot there were three lanes; a left turning lane, a middle lane to drive straight, and a right hand turning lane. The store she worked at was a truck stop that would allow semi-trucks to stay overnight, take showers, and do whatever was necessary to be rested. So as I am in the right hand lane to turn right out of the parking lot, a semi-truck is also trying to turn right but he didn't have his blinker on. Once the coast was clear he pulled out and begins to drag the truck I was in down the road with him! I'm screaming inside the truck, blowing the horn, and needless to say I'm terrified! Finally, something in me spoke and said jump out, so I opened the passenger door and jumped out while the truck was being taken down the road. He must have felt something pulling because he finally stopped driving to notice that he was dragging another truck down the road. The guy driving had the nerve to be mad with me when he was found to be in the wrong. He began cursing and spitting. Again, God never intended to kill me. The assignment He has me on has never been about me, ever! Humbly dear God, I thank You! The truck was a total loss and from that day to this one, I cannot tell you what happened with that truck. Jason, however, was furious!   My sister was crying, I was crying, and I just wanted to sit down and smoke a joint. Fast forward a couple months later; Jason started to trust me again because he could see that I was all about making my money. He asked me to come ride somewhere with him which was not out of the ordinary. We went up Hwy 40 on the dirt roads to a house way in the back of the housing sub division. It took forever to get there. When we finally arrived at the destination; he was like "come on" and turned the car off and took the keys. When we got out, I could smell dog crap and wet grass. Inside the house were two young kids. Look like they were no more than age seven and ten. There was also a young baby maybe six months or so. A girl about my sister's age emerged from the back as well. She asked "what do you want to eat?" It didn't take me long to figure out that this was a girl he was dating or something. She didn't speak and I didn't either. I really just wanted to get out of there. He went in the back and did whatever it was he went there to do and then we left. Once in the car, I didn't ask who she was and I really didn't care and he didn't volunteer anything which was fine with me. We lived by a "don't ask don't tell" kind of life which is why we got along so well. He and my sister found out they were pregnant not long after that and I couldn't be happier. She eventually delivered the baby and named him after a friend of hers because she was upset with Jason. After the dust had settled and some legal matters had washed over, she proceeded to file the paperwork to change my nephew's name. I, by this time, had found a very good job at a mortgage company and was finally doing something with my life. Life looked promising. Then, in one weekend it all changed. I was planning to throw a Passion party for women to purchase exotic toys. My cousin whom I lived next to on the prison grounds years earlier had re-emerged. She called me to tell me she would stop by to see me on her way to Jacksonville for the weekend and asked me if I wanted to go. I really wanted to go because I had never been to Jacksonville but I was supposed to be throwing a party that same night. She said "well think about and I will stop by your house in a few hours". I had brought all of the stuff for the party; food, drinks, invited over 40 people, decorated, however; I wanted to go to Jacksonville. My cousin arrived at my house as promised and saw all of the decorations and asked me what was going on. I explained to her I was supposed to be throwing a party. She asked "are you going or not?" I was like "come on" and gathered up as much of the food that I could carry and a bag of clothes and off to Jacksonville we went. The first night there we linked up with a good friend of hers, got dressed and headed out for the club. Once we pulled up, the first thing that I noticed is that it was packed. We got out and walked in without paying which was a little different because I'd never went in a club for free. It wasn't until the next set of doors flew open that I realize that this was a strip club. It was so loud and filled with weed smoke and half naked females. She told me to sit down and that she would be back. When I saw her again she had a bag on her arm, a cup in one hand, and a cigarette in the other hand. She asked "do you want to dance?" I replied "are you serious?" I was so hesitant and nervous and had a heck of lot of emotions running through me. She said "I can give you something to wear." "The first time I danced, I was nervous also, but stop being so scary!" she went on to say. I was like "alright, I'm in". She took me in the back and gave me what look like a two-piece bathing suit and some of the highest heels I had ever seen. I put on my outfit and turned and looked in the mirror and really didn't know what to think. I had worn a two-piece before but never with heels and certainly never in a strip club. My heart was pounding out of my chest! She said "okay, come on". On the inside, I felt like I was dying. She grabbed my hand and out of the dressing room we went. She proceeded to give me my instructions on how to approach the person. "You just walk up to them and ask them if they want a dance". As simple as it sounded, it was the craziest thing I had ever heard and I refused to ask one person but somehow at the end of the night, I walked out of there with nearly $450.00 after three hours. The next night it was the same routine but somehow, I felt a little more comfortable than the night before. The next morning when I woke up and counted my money I had close to $1000.00 for less than two days. I had just stumbled on something that would be my life for the next four years. I got back home Sunday night, took a shower and laid in my bed to think about what had just happened. The next morning I went to work to The Mortgage Company. Every morning, it was the same routine for me; head to work early to get a good parking spot and call Jason to see what was on the agenda after I got off. I called him on the morning of February 16th 2006 but I didn't get an answer. I tried again and again but still no answer. I blew it off and figured he was still asleep and had probably just laid down at some girl's house (knowing him). There was also a concert that night and performing was an old friend of me and my sisters and I wanted to go. I needed to ask my mom if she could watch my son and I would come back and get him the next day. I called her but when she answered, it was a cry on the other end of the phone like I had never heard before. I've known her all my life and I've heard her cry before but I have never heard one in this tone. She said to me "something is wrong with Coreyon, they can't get him to breathe" and I said "HUH" and paused and said "Who can't get him to breathe?" She said "Your cousin and Jason, they can't get him to breathe, call her" When I called my cousin, as soon as she picked up it was again a cry that I had never heard before, she was hysterical! I kept asking her "what's wrong, what's wrong". She finally said sobbing "Carra, I can't get him to breathe. I can't get him to breathe". Because I am still in shock I asked "WHO?" Sobbing she said "JC". My heart sank! This is the child I have been helping my sister raise. I had already lost a child due to an abortion. This is the child who was at my house more than my own child. This is the child that my son considered his brother instead of his first cousin. I was in the delivery room when this child was born! I was often up with him at night with my sister. JESUS! I finally asked "where are you?" She wouldn't answer, only sobbed. I asked again "where are you?" Again no answer, only sobs. She finally said "we are at Jason's house. I said "call the ambulance". "I can't" she replied. I said "call mama" (referring to my mom). She said "I can't." I told her I would call her back and hung up to call my mom. When my mom answered, I told her what my cousin had told me and she said "tell her to call the ambulance or take him to the hospital." I hung up with her and called my cousin back. When she answered I relayed the message my mom had given me to give her and again she refused. The messaging back and forth went on for the better part of 30 to 45 minutes. I really didn't understand the severity of the issue. I was totally naïve to the circumstances at hand. In the back of my mind; I was also very fearful of losing the first real job I had ever had. It was only when I tried to call my cousin and she didn't answer when I got up the courage to tell my boss I had a family emergency and had to go. When I got to Jason's house, there was no one there. I called my mom and she advised to come to the hospital. When I arrived at the hospital, I told the receptionist that I believe my nephew was just brought in and gave her his name. The somber look on her face is one I will never forget. She simply pointed to the locked double doors and told me she would buzz me in. When the doors flung open, the first face I saw was my mom's tear soaked face and she said "THEY KILLED MY BABY" over and over and over again. I will never forget those words or her tone. Just like that, his life was gone at the age of 6. The autopsy described his death as "trauma to the torso". The Examiner stated the damages was like an adult in a car wearing a seatbelt at 70 mph going head on into a tree. I slid down the wall I was leaning on and wailed very loudly.

Chapter 5

Not In Vain

I called my sister and as she answered, I was crying and told her "he's dead". She had no knowledge anything was wrong at all. It's in times like this where even the Holiest person must wonder, why? Even if the word never leaves your lips, you have to wonder why? God does everything in His perfect timing because He is perfect. Absolutely perfect! With my heart now ripped out of my chest and not fully knowing the word of God, I knew there had to be a celebration of his life. At the coroner's office days later; my mom, a good friend of my mom, and myself went to see his body because they wouldn't allow us to see him at the hospital. My mom asked if I really wanted to see him. My mind was settled on the fact that I had to see him. We walked in and the room was so cold. There he was lying on a cold table uncovered from the neck up. I could not hold back the tears. The coroner asked if we wanted to see the bruises on him and before my mom could open her mouth I said "YES" crying. She pulled the cover back that was over his body which revealed the "Y" that was cut down his torso. She pointed out the bruises across the crown of his head, the edges of his face, across his chest and I wailed and wailed and cried so hard. I prayed for him aloud and told him to be good up there and I kissed his cheek. His body was so cold, I would've never guessed it would be that cold. Months earlier, Jason and my cousin had started a public relationship which is why she was at his house so often. I can't recall which one but one of them asked me what I thought about their relationship in the beginning and I told them then that "nothing good can come of this". Although I was consumed in sin; I didn't think a public relationship would be a very good idea. After all, he did have a child by my sister. There was something that was said at "JC's" funeral by the Pastor that I'll never forget. He said to the audience "don't let the death of this child to be in vain". At that very moment a light clicked on in my head. It was at that very moment I kind of felt my life wouldn't be the same. I mourned his death for a very long time. I had never experienced a death so close and personal. In order to release the unexplained emotions that I was feeling internally; I tried to physically fight my uncle who was a former boxing champ as well as ex-military knowing there was no way I would have won that fight. I told my son, but because he was so young (6 to be exact), I knew he didn't fully understand. I explained it to the best of my ability. I told him his cousin had gone to live with God and that he wouldn't be able to play with him anymore. He looked at me and said "I don't want him to go there; I want him to play with me". It seemed as if I couldn't stop crying throughout the night. At the trial, the judge sentenced Jason to life without the possibility of parole plus 30 more years for Capital Murder. Jason and I had been through so much together. I knew at the trial I had to tell the truth about what I knew about him as a person, regardless of what the charges against him stated. "I knew him to be a very loving father, he has a lot of kids in different states and I've never known him to discipline his kids to the point of abuse, he loved those kids" I testified. In all honesty, it was at this point in my life I started to feel a pull in my spirit. I begin to hear a voice in my head that was not mine. The Voice would talk to me and show me my enemies and tell me when I shouldn't go and do the stuff that I had always loved; drugs, partying and hanging out. I would try and ignore this Voice but it would get stronger and stronger and stronger. I also begin to see visions of things before they would happen. I had a dream I was sitting at a table talking to a guy that looked like God. He was very peaceful and patient and He held my hand. I can't hear the words we were saying but the picture was clear as day and I was still mourning. After the sentencing, I felt empty for the longest time. My six year old nephew was gone and I had lost what I felt like was one of my best friends, Jason. I was very upset with everyone because of what happened. I felt like everyone was involved. During this time, my relationship with my sister was not the best and my relationship with my cousin went from good to horrible. I didn't want to speak with her or be around her at all. I feel as if information was being withheld so I stayed to myself for the most part. I guess you can say I was in a state of depression. When I should've been talking to God I was eating ecstasy pills in the strip club. Just when I was at the point of giving up; God stepped in. I understand then and now that God makes no mistakes and that He is very intentional. I can only thank Him every day for what happened. To my nephew, until we meet again auntie baby, I love you always and you are my inspiration forever. Coreyon Armani "JC" Graham *June 12, 2000 - February 16, 2006*.

Chapter 6

"Tip Out"

After I was able to shake the mourning state I was in, it was back to the strip club I went. When I should have been thanking and praising God, I was eating ecstasy pills and taking trips across Florida. If you didn't know what I had just been through, you would've never known by my behavior that I just experienced the most traumatic time of my life. Every year for Memorial Day, a group of friends and myself would go to Miami for the Memorial Day holiday. I knew just what I was going to do, I wanted to go and dance. I never would go to Miami by myself though because that is just not one of those places you visit alone. As soon as we got there, we went to our hotel and checked in and out the door we would go. I really never stayed in one of the extravagant hotels on South Beach because I was not there on vacation, I was there working. My very first time to Miami was with a friend girl I use to work with. She moved to Ocala to get away from the "city life" as she called it but went back home frequently and asked me if I wanted to go one weekend. I was all in! That night I told her that I danced and wanted to check out a few clubs and she was more than glad to take me because her sister in Miami danced as well. When we got to the club at about 1am, it was packed! Wall to wall, door to door! We walked in and I asked to speak to the manager about dancing that night. He asks me "you from Miami?" I said no. He said "out of town girls is $75.00 a night!" This almost blew my socks off because the clubs back home was only $45.00. Every strip club has a "tip out" fee that you must pay before dancing or before you leave that is given to the DJ to play the music. I turned and looked at my friend girl and she said "my sister has worked here before, you're sure to make your money back." I looked at the manager and said okay. He then said "and you have to be completely nude by the end of the first song". This again completely shocked me because I had never been nude before. Back home, we were not allowed to take anything off. Here in Miami, their slots are 3 songs a piece. I asked him "So you mean I have to dance nude for 2 whole songs?" He answered "are you on or not?" I again looked at my friend and she reassured me it would be okay and I agreed. It was show time! That night I made the most money I had ever made dancing. When we left the club it was in the wee hours of the morning possibly 5 or 6am as the sun was coming up. I had never been to the club all night before. It was a rush. During the day; I would work weekdays at my fulltime job at the Mortgage Company and dance all night on the weekends going from city to city. When we left Miami that weekend, I was already thinking of when and who I would go back with. My friend girl that I went with told me on the way back about the Memorial Day bash as well. It was on! When I got back home I told a group of girls that I use to travel with about my experience and we not long after that planned our trip to go back. The really weird thing about my life of sin is that it never felt comfortable for me; it just made me the money that I needed to do the things I loved; shopping, drugs and tattoos. It came time for us to leave and go back to Miami and we had no money, literally. But we were able to hustle up just enough money to get to Miami and off we went. We weren't worried about what we were going to do or where we would sleep, because we figured we would find somewhere. Soon as we touched down I took her to the club I danced at and just like before, the guy read her the rules; however she wasn't interested in nude dancing. She sat the night out but off to the stage I went. Just like the prior trip, I made a ton of money. We ended up staying about three or four days and then went back home. It was the times I was home alone that God would speak to me. I didn't know at that time that that was the voice of the Lord and honestly I wasn't trying to find out. I was actually too afraid to tell anyone because I thought they would think I was crazy or just high. But as crazy as it sounds, He would talk to me then also. Inside, I knew I wasn't supposed to be doing those things but the devil made it so attractive. Fast forward a year or so and it finally came to the point that I was just tired of it all. I had been to jail, been through so much strife and turmoil, and I wanted out. I just wanted out.

Chapter 7
I Surrendered!

I called my Aunt because she was on the leadership board of the church that I've went to since I was a child and told her I wanted to give my life to Christ. That is actually the first time I've actually wanted to go to church since I was an adult. Growing up, we didn't have an option. Sunday, Monday, Tuesday, Thursday and Friday we were at church. If the Pastor called a revival on Saturday, we were there too. I was raised Pentecostal. Growing up, the church we worshipped in looked like a 1 bedroom house without the walls separating the room from the living room and it had a tin roof. It would be packed from wall to wall with hardly anywhere to sit if you got there late. The pews were not the nice ones and didn't have cushion like the ones now a days. I had been out of church for so long that I didn't even know we had moved from that location into a mansion of a church not far away. When she told me to meet her and our missionary (she's our Apostle now) at the new sanctuary, I only had two questions: 1. what is a sanctuary and 2. Where is it at? I had been out of church so long that I wasn't aware the sanctuary was the actual church. I got the directions from her and just as she had asked, I met them at the sanctuary. When I finally saw the church it was huge and was twenty times bigger than our former church. I was amazed. I went inside and sat on one of the pews which even had cushion, I was simply in awe. I sat and waited on my aunt and after 45 minutes I decided I was going to leave. I said to myself "this is crazy". She never called and I was sure she had simply forgotten. As I was walking out to exit the same glass doors I used to enter I ran into the missionary. She looked at me and said "where were you" I said "waiting in there, I've been in there for 45 minutes" she said "Lord, you were waiting on God" and grabbed me by my hand and took me into her office which is where my aunt was. She asked me to sit down and asked me why did I want to be saved? I told her "I felt so empty and something was missing from my life and I don't know what it is." She then came and laid her hands on my head and said "it's the Lord you are missing" and her and my aunt begin to pray and speak in tongues which lasted for about 10 minutes. I felt as if a weight had been lifted off of me. Missionary looked at me and said "don't go back". She said "you are going to have to cut off all ties to your past in order to fully walk with the Lord". When I left there I felt so free. I immediately threw all of the rap and R& B music in my car out the window. I no longer had a desire to listen to it. I headed to grab a bite to eat and was still crying from what had just happened at the church. I wasn't crying from hurt but from the Power of God. It was the most amazing feeling that I had ever felt in my life. After I ate, I went home and went to sleep. A week later, my cousin came by my apartment to hang out and I told her what had happened at the church and she begin to catch me up on what I had missed in my old world. Looking back, I should have asked her to leave because missionary had just told me I would have to cut off all ties to my past. But this was my cousin! She surely couldn't have meant her? I continued to allow my cousin to visit whenever she wanted to, and I was at her house where we use to hang out at when I was "in my sin" whenever I wanted to. I can recall the first time I had ever been broke after accepting Christ. I had a job making about $16.00 an hour which was good money back then and I was going to church faithfully. I didn't have my hair done which I normally would do weekly. I had one more meal that I could cook before I would have to ask for food and I only had gas to get home from work that day. Just like with every other check; I had already paid my tithe and gave my offering and was broke after bills. No one had a clue that I was broke. After work that day I crank my car up and went straight home. To pass my house, I had to pass my mailbox so I stopped and checked my mail and the last piece of mail I saw was a letter from a known check distributor. I opened the letter and attached was a check for $800.00. My hands begin to shake and I yelled as loud as I could. That was the first time I personally saw the power of God. The next day I came home and stopped and checked the mail and it was another letter with a check attached for $950.00. The next day I came home and check the mail and there was another letter with a check attached for $500.00. The day after that was pay day at work. When I came home after work that Friday I was completely overwhelmed after I sat and thought about the days prior. I walked around the house alone praying and crying out to God. I was so overwhelmed because I had never seen anything like that. When I sat down trying to compose myself, tears would just fall and I found myself walking around again praying and crying. An hour or so later I found myself kneeling beside my son's empty bed (he was at his dad's house for the weekend) crying and praying, praying and crying for another 30 minutes just giving thanks at times. With my eyes closed, it looked as if someone had turned the light on in my son's room. This was strange because I was home alone and the lights were off inside my apartment. When I opened my eyes, I saw a white light so bright that I had to close my eyes because it actually scared me. When I opened my eyes back again, the light was gone. I got up and walked around my apartment to check and make sure no one was there. I knew it wasn't, but I needed to check. I've wondered since that day if this was Jesus or an Angel wanting to talk to me? I didn't tell a living soul about this experience until years later in July, 2015.

Chapter 8

Backslidden

I honestly can't tell you what made me slide back into the world but I can tell you that I take full responsibility as I've never been one to shift the blame. I was still working at TBW and had even made a new friend name "Courtney" who would later be someone I would go through another traumatic experience with. I was actually going to Jacksonville the same weekend I met her but I could tell she was not the same caliber female as I was. She looked to be a very "good girl" and we already know how I was living. Once I backslid back into the world, it was like I had to make up for lost times. I did tell her at work that I was going to Jacksonville and asked if she wanted to go. Of course she wanted to know why I was going and although I was a little hesitant about telling her, I told her the truth. "I am going to dance". She replied "really?" "Yes" I responded. She laughed in disbelief. Dancing was not as big as it is now a days so the people in the town where I am from did it discreetly. She said "I don't want to do that" and I told her "you don't have to, its people in the club who don't dance at all they just go to drink and chill" and she said "okay". When we got off work, our bags were already in the car and we hit the highway headed to Jacksonville. I called a good friend of mine named "LeLe" and told her I was on my way and that I had someone with me. She asked "who?" and I told her it was a chick from work. We never invited outside females into our circle, it was just a no-no. "Are you for real?" She said "you gone lose your job, she gone tell on you!" I assured her that Courtney was cool and that we would see her in a bit. After I hung up I had to be sure Courtney was as cool as I had just said she was. I said to Courtney "what goes on Jacksonville stays in Jacksonville". She laughed and said of course. We turned the music up and put the pedal to the metal. Once we pulled up in Jacksonville and turned the car off, LeLe came outside to greet me. She gave me a hug, looked over in the passenger seat at Courtney and said "girl, she is white!" I laughed and Courtney said "hi" very casually. We got out and went inside where LeLe and I begin to talk about what club we were going to. The sun begins to fall and we begin to get dressed to head out. We got in the car and headed to the club but half way there I remembered I left 1 of my shoes so we ended up having to turn round. Back at LeLe's house I ran upstairs to get my shoes and ate another ecstasy pill. I sit and think every day about how I'm supposed to be dead from all of the pill use. It would be to the point of six and seven a night on some nights. Again, I really feel it was never apart of God's plan that I would die. To a certain degree, He wasn't concerned about the sin. It's the souls that would be saved as a result of the life I was living. He knew eventually he would snatch me out and speak life into a broken, brittle, lifeless corpse of a body that I was living in. I've also always wondered out of all the billions of people in this world that we live in why did he choose me? The dark skinned girl with the big teeth that was picked on in school. I will forever be indebted to Him. I owe Him so much more than what He is requiring of me. Without Him, I surely would have died from either an overdose or the streets. If you're reading this and the stories in this book are speaking directly to you, please know that your life will impact nations one day soon. He is calling you out of your secret places. Once you surrender completely, things in your life will begin to make sense.

Now at the seasoned age of 33, I have a successful business as a Motivational Speaker and Life Coach speaking to the same people from my past. Although the youth, women and men that I speak to I've actually never met before personally, their faces, lives and stories I know all too well as I was living that way once in my life. I heard my Apostle said once "it's so weird when you see someone living like you once did and it bothers you. You can't really get mad because again that was you at one point." Is it wrong to say that it use to disgusts me a little and that I was little embarrassed at my past? I just remind myself that God delivered me from that so there is no reason to be ashamed or embarrassed, I don't live there anymore so I just thank him daily. I am so grateful. There is actually a lot more to my story so stay tuned because part II will soon follow. Be blessed!

Toccarra James – President and Founder of Gods Servant Empowered Me Inc.

www.ingramcontent.com/pod-product-compliance
Lightning Source LLC
Chambersburg PA
CBHW061200040426
42445CB00013B/1757